W9-BON-835

HOW DID THEY BUILD THAT?

One World Trade Center

RAMANDEEP KAUR

How Did They Build That? One World Trade Center

Copyright © 2016
Published by Scobre Educational
Written by Ramandeep Kaur

Scobre Educational
2255 Calle Clara
La Jolla, CA 92037

Scobre Operations & Administration
42982 Osgood Road
Fremont, CA 94539

www.scobre.com
info@scobre.com

Scobre Educational publications may be purchased for
educational, business, or sales promotional use.

Cover design by Sara Radka
Layout design by Nicole Ramsay
Edited by Michelle Lee
Photos thanks to Newscom, iStockPhoto, and Shutterstock

ISBN: 978-1-62920-555-7 (Library Bound)
ISBN: 978-1-62920-554-0 (eBook)

INDEX

INTRODUCTION

With its crowds of people, music, fashion, and art scene, New York City is a place ripe with new sights, new wonders, and of course, big things. The famous city **skyline** is filled with some of the tallest **skyscrapers** in the world.

One of those buildings is One World Trade Center. At 1,776 feet, it is the tallest building in the United States. The height is a reminder of the Declaration of Independence which was signed in 1776 when America declared its freedom from Great Britain.

One World Trade Center is made from concrete, steel, and glass. It is rectangular in shape with a triangular front that reaches to the top of the building. The

One World Trade Center stands 1,176 feet high.

skyscraper starts off wide and slowly becomes thinner until it looks like there is a needle at the very top. The blue-green glass makes the building glitter for miles around.

The building is used as office space. It has more than 100 floors, world-class restaurants, a museum in front, and a stunning view from the top. The building **structure** is **environmentally friendly** because it saves energy and is made from recycled materials.

Another important fact about One World Trade Center is that it is not the first World Trade Center. The first one had seven buildings, including the famous Twin Towers. However, they were destroyed during the September 11 attacks in 2001. After clearing all the rubble, the World Trade Center was rebuilt and One World Trade Center was born. Also called the "Freedom Tower," One World Trade Center is a **symbol** of America's strength after difficult times.

HISTORY

Construction on the original World Trade Center began on August 5, 1966 and it opened on April 4, 1973. It was home to seven buildings but two of them stood out from the rest. These two buildings looked the same in size and appearance. They were known as the North and South Towers, or the Twin Towers.

The Twin Towers were well known in New York City and even held the record of being the tallest buildings in the world from 1971 to 1973. Unfortunately, they were destroyed on September 11, 2001. Terrorists took control of two airplanes and flew them into the buildings. Both towers collapsed and thousands of people died. The date of the disaster is

A view of the New York City skyline with the original World Trade Center.

symbolic because it happened on 9/11. This date reminds everyone that the attacks were a serious emergency to the American people. Hundreds of police officers and firefighters came to save people who were trapped in the building. Some of them gave up their lives to save others and are remembered as heroes.

The damage to the World Trade Center was terrible and it took about eight months to clean and save the remains. The other five buildings that were a part of the World Trade Center were also severely damaged. Those buildings had to be destroyed in order to make new structures.

After the September 11 attacks, plans to rebuild the World Trade Center began and it was decided that there would be six new skyscrapers. **Construction** of One World Trade Center began on April 27, 2006. It was made to be a memorial for the lives lost during the 9/11 attacks.

After the building was finished, all that remained was creating the spire. A spire is a cone-shaped structure that is placed on top of the roof of a building. A spire helps a building become taller and it also makes it look unique and beautiful. As a symbol of American freedom, the builders wanted One World Trade Center to stand out above the rest.

The spire is 408 feet tall and gives One World Trade Center its iconic height of 1,776 feet. Before One World Trade Center, was built the Empire State Building was the tallest skyscraper in New York City. Now One World Trade Center holds the record of being the tallest building in the United States and the fourth tallest in the world.

During construction of this building, many New Yorkers were afraid that the new World Trade Center would make people forget the 9/11 attacks and the former glory of the original World Trade Center. The Twin Towers were an

The destruction of the 9/11 attacks

Two bright lights show where the Twin Towers once stood while the new One World Trade Center can be seen on the right.

important part of the New York City skyline and millions of people from all over the world came to visit them. Because of this, it was important to New Yorkers that One World Trade Center did not replace the Twin Towers or look very similar to them.

Instead, a whole different look and style was created for the building. One World Trade Center would have a one-of-a-kind design, environmentally friendly features, and special safety mechanisms. The unique difference of One World Trade Center allows the building to begin its own exciting history, but traces of the past are still very present in the building. One World Trade Center stands only a few hundred feet from where the original Twin Towers stood and it also commemorates the 9/11 attacks with the National September 11 Memorial and Museum right in front of it.

DID YOU KNOW?
Firefighters, police officers, and other emergency workers helped save 25,000 people before the Twin Towers collapsed.

TIMELINE

The Construction Timeline of One World Trade Center

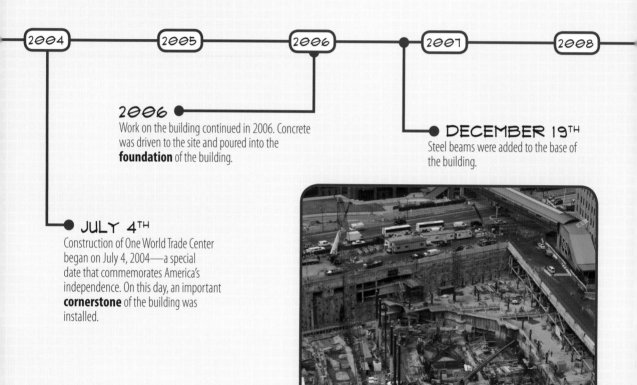

| 2004 | 2005 | 2006 | 2007 | 2008 |

2006
Work on the building continued in 2006. Concrete was driven to the site and poured into the **foundation** of the building.

DECEMBER 19TH
Steel beams were added to the base of the building.

JULY 4TH
Construction of One World Trade Center began on July 4, 2004—a special date that commemorates America's independence. On this day, an important **cornerstone** of the building was installed.

The steel base of One World Trade Center

2010
Glass began to be installed on the 20th floor of the tower.

DEC. 16TH
One World Trade Center surpassed 600 feet in height.

2012
One World Trade Center was completed up to the roof level. After this point, one of the beams was signed by President Barack Obama, State of New York officials, and construction workers.

2009 — **2010** — **2011** — **2012** — **2013**

2012
Toward the end of 2012, pieces of the steel spire were brought from Canada to New York. The installation of the spire took place over several months.

2013
Construction moved to the outside of the building. Workers began building the plaza that would surround One World Trade Center.

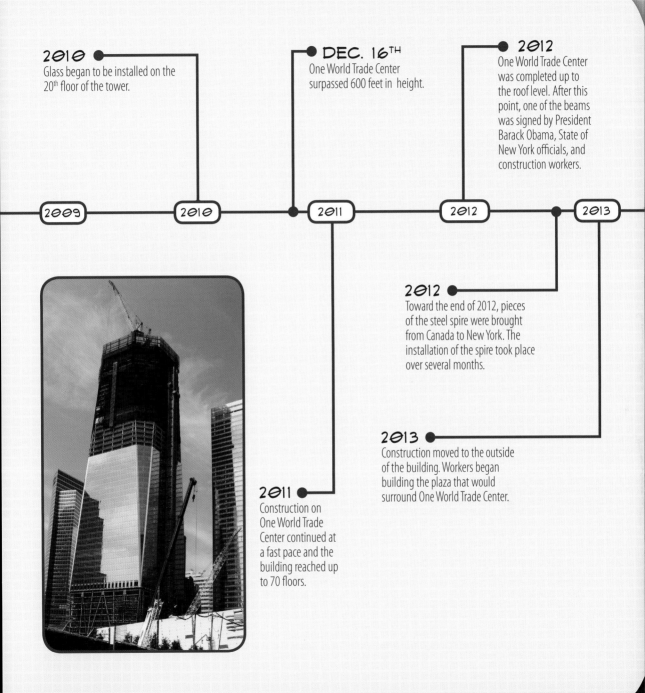

2011
Construction on One World Trade Center continued at a fast pace and the building reached up to 70 floors.

LOCATION

There are many great skyscrapers in New York, but One World Trade Center is more than just another building to New Yorkers. Many of them are haunted by the **tragedy** of 9/11 and the collapse of the Twin Towers. Because of the people's fears, builders made sure that the new World Trade Center is more safe and secure.

One World Trade Center has wide staircases that give people plenty of room to escape if there is an emergency. Before, the Twin Towers had narrow staircases, and many stairways were blocked when the building began to collapse. Now One World Trade Center is strengthened so that it will not easily collapse in another disaster. There are also many backup features, such as emergency lighting and safety systems built into the walls. These safety features give New Yorkers a much-needed sense of security.

DID YOU KNOW?
Other famous buildings in New York City are the Empire State Building, the Chrysler Building, and the Statue of Liberty.

New York City at sunrise, with a view of One World Trade Center (right) and the Statue of Liberty (left)

PURPOSE

One World Trade Center is used as office space by many different companies. Beijing Vantone Industrial was the first company to have a spot at the new building. This company is dedicated to helping those in need. Throughout the years, Vantone has helped raise money for disaster relief efforts, environmental protection, and books for education. Their "Vantone China Center" is scheduled to be located between floors 64 and 69.

Another well known company that will be taking space in the building is Condé Nast Publications. Condé Nast Publications is responsible for publishing the magazines *Glamour*,

One World Trade Center has some offices dedicated to fashion.

GQ, *Vogue*, and *Wired*. In a city prized for its art and high sense of fashion, it makes sense that One World Trade Center would be home to many popular magazines. Condé Nast will take over one million square feet in the building between floors 20 to 44.

The building is also used as a tourist attraction. Visitors can dine in the fine restaurants or view all of New York from the tallest building in the nation.

DID YOU KNOW?
One World Trade Center is so tall that you can even see all the way to New Jersey on a clear day.

MATERIALS

Many materials were used to create One World Trade Center and an important one is steel. Steel makes up the framework of the building. Without it, the

building would not be able to stand on its own. There are heavy pieces of steel underneath the building and also around it. To create the **perimeter** of the building, 24 steel columns were needed and they were 59 feet long and more than 141,095 pounds each. The large amount of steel proves how sturdy and strong building material has to be. It is estimated that the completed One World Trade Center will be made from 40,000 tons of steel.

Other materials in the building are concrete and glass. The glass windows give One World Trade Center its sparkling glow while the concrete is also strong material. Concrete is a mix of cement, sand, and water and hardens to any shape that the builder wants. When combined, steel, concrete, and glass make a strong and beautiful structure that will last for a long time.

DID YOU KNOW?

One World Trade Center uses 49,000 cubic yards of concrete. That's enough concrete to make a 200-mile-long sidewalk.

Construction workers work on completing the top of One World Trade Center.

FEATURES

A unique part of One World Trade Center is the National September 11 Memorial & Museum, which is right in front of the building. Visitors come from around the world to pay their respects to fallen citizens and heroes.

The **memorial** section of the museum is a peaceful place in the middle of the buzzing city. It has many lush trees which surround two square pools. The pools are located where the Twin Towers used to be and the names of the 9/11 victims are written on the walls around them.

The museum opened to the public on May 21, 2014. Inside the museum, there are up to 23,000 images and 10,300 artifacts relating to the 9/11 attacks. This allows people to view an important part of American history that is remembered and honored every day.

DID YOU KNOW?

In the memorial exhibit of the museum, there is a hallway covered with nearly 3,000 photographs of men, women, and children who died as a result of the 9/11 attacks. Visitors can learn more about each person through additional photos and audio recordings from family, friends, and co-workers.

The 9/11 Memorial at Ground Zero, Lower Manhattan

HIGHLIGHTS

A WRAP-AROUND GLASS FRONT

When you first look up at One World Trade Center, there is a glass front that wraps around the building. This glass is not ordinary as it is resistant to bomb blasts. Not only is the glass useful to the building, but it also adds to its beauty. It contains a smaller tint of green and is made to sparkle in the daylight. The reflective glass gives the building a lively look and the glittering tower can be seen by all who walk through

ENVIRONMENTALLY FRIENDLY

About eighty percent of the building is created from recycled waste materials. With its smooth surface and perfect edges, it is hard to believe the material was once made from trash! This shows how the makers of the building were dedicated to the well being of the environment from the very beginning of construction. The building also saves energy by using fewer electric lights and more natural lighting. The steam that comes out of the building is not wasted, but used to power the building, and there are storage tanks on the 57th floor that are used to collect rainwater.

ter

A BOMB-PROOF BASE

When the plans to build One World Trade Center began, the creators wanted to make the building powerful and secure. To create a nearly **indestructible** building, a **bombproof** base was created. The base is so powerful that it can tolerate the strength and violence of a 1,500-pound truck bomb. To make the building look attractive, the bombproof base is covered in reflective glass that hides the power that One World Trade Center truly holds.

A $3.9 BILLION MONUMENT

It is estimated that the total cost of the skyscraper was $3.9 billion. About $1 billion was paid for by Silverstein Properties as insurance money because of the destruction of the original World Trade Center. The Port Authority provided another $1 billion and the State of New York kindly donated $250 million to the construction.

SIMILAR STRUCTURES

EMPIRE STATE BUILDING

From 1931 to 1970, the Empire State Building was the tallest building in the world. When One World Trade Center was built, the Empire State Building became the second tallest building in New York City.

BANK OF AMERICA TOWER

The Bank of America Tower is the third tallest building in New York City. It is often compared to One World Trade Center because of its award-winning environmentally friendly design.

WILLIS TOWER

The Willis Tower is located in Chicago, Illinois and was completed in 1973. From 1973 to 1998, it held the record for being the tallest building in the world.

TAIPEI 101

Taipei 101 is located in Taipei, Taiwan, and was ranked as the tallest building in the world from 2004 to 2010. When Dubai's skyscraper Burj Khalifa opened in 2010, Taipei 101 lost the title of being the tallest skyscraper in the world.

PEOPLE

The main **architects** of One World Trade Center were David Childs and Daniel Libeskind. For Libeskind, becoming the master plan architect for one of the most famous buildings in the world was not an easy process. In order to be chosen, Libeskind had to enter a competition with people from all over the world.

When he won, Libekind went to work at designing the building. He was the one who planned out the height of the building at 1,776 feet, however many of his other ideas did not make it to the final design. Many people

Daniel Libeskind, left, and David Childs, right, are responsible for creating One World Trade Center.

thought that the planned building was not strong enough to survive another terrorist attack and so David Childs took over the rest of the plan. Childs was responsible for designing the wide staircases, safety systems, and bombproof base. From the way One World Trade Center looks today, its stylish look, environmentally friendly design, and safety features make it a one-of-a-kind building.

DID YOU KNOW?
One World Trade Center is the largest environmentally friendly building in the world.

IMPACT

Tourists who travel to Lower Manhattan can visit One World Trade Center and ride the elevators. The elevators are fast and can deliver people to the top in 60 seconds. That's almost two floors per second!

At the top is an observation deck called One World Observatory. The deck is three acres in size, so there is plenty of room for visitors to crowd together at the top and see all the sights of New York City. In fact, if you are lucky enough to visit One World Trade Center on a clear day, you can see places from up to 50 miles away.

Already cherished by the United States as the "Freedom Tower," the building will soon be the heart of New York City. Over time, it will be accessible by dozens of subway lines and transportation centers—drawing crowds of people for an unforgettable view at the top of the building, a walk back in time as they step through the National September 11 Museum, and a chance to dine at one of the greatest buildings in the world.

Sky view of downtown Manhattan and New Jersey. From One World Trade Center, you can see all the way to New Jersey.

GLOSSARY

architect: a person who designs buildings and other structures

bombproof: something strong enough to withstand the force of a bomb

construction: the process of building something

cornerstone: a stone representing the starting place of an important building

environmentally friendly: an adjective that describes something good or healthy for the environment

foundation: the base or ground on which a building stands

indestructible: something that cannot be destroyed

memorial: something made to remember a person or event

perimeter: the outer walls or frame of a building

skyline: the outline of buildings against the sky

skyscraper: a very tall building with many floors, usually for office use

structure: something that is built or constructed, like a building, house, or bridge

symbol: something that represents something else

tragedy: a sad or tragic event, usually involving death